MOVING FORWARD

Joe Joe and Autumn Dawson

TABLE OF CONTENTS

CHAPTER 1: OUTRUNNING YOUR PAST

Moving Forward! As we dive into this book together, I hope that as you read these pages you become excited and encouraged to move forward in every area of your life. This has become one of my life messages. I will speak on moving forward all the days of my life. As a person grows closer to God, they also grow closer to their personal identity. When someone knows who they are in God, they become an unstoppable force.

Through this book, I want to help equip and train you to always keep your personal relationship with God alive and fresh. As you learn how to commune with the Lord, in a very real way, He will always guide you and lead you into the deeper purposes He has for you. Through these pages, I pray that the Holy Spirit will reveal key insights for your life to spur you forward constantly and keep you continually moving in the areas God has directed you into.

When the Lord first started to speak to me about moving forward, He said, "I want you to move aggressively forward in every area of your life. Move aggressively forward in life, family, ministry and business." Now is the time to move forward aggressively into all God has called you to do. The reason people get frustrated in life and with life is because they quit moving forward. You simply have to move forward in every area of your life. Truth be told, we never really plateau in life, we are either moving forward or backward. Our spiritual nature and our physical nature have a lot in common. When you quit working on an area, you begin to lose ground and become weak in those particular areas.

When someone stops going to the gym, they never keep their size or shape. If a guy is trying to bulk up, they will lose muscle mass and begin to gain weight the wrong way. If someone is trying to lose weight and watches what they eat, has a good cardio regiment but then leaves the gym, they will start to gain the unwanted weight back.

It's the same way spiritually. When someone is reading the word, praying, journaling, watching and listening to the right material, they are moving forward. But when they stop, those moments and times are filled with other things. They may not necessarily be in sin, but they stop growing spiritually. There are only two directions in life, forward or backward. If we don't consciously focus on moving forward, we will find ourselves moving backward.

If someone is an entrepreneur an idea, and they come against some resistance or a roadblock, they have two choices. They can either stop and give up all of the forward momentum they have gained or they can choose to keep going and plow right over or through the obstacle before them. When God has given you a dream or project to work on, you must understand there will always be opposition. But always remember that God is far greater than anything that tries to stop you from moving forward.

Many times, we need to gain more wisdom and understanding in certain areas before we enter into the next stage of the process. God will put the right people and training in front of us to help equip us to move past the current barriers we face. To move forward in any ministry, business, or life endeavor, you must always be training and gaining insight for what is coming in the next season. When we stay forever a student, Jesus is faithful to stay our forever teacher.

God wants to make a deposit of clarity into our lives. That deposit of clarity will speak peace and calm to the storm that has been raging. Clarity will always drive out fear and bring peace. Right now, even as you sit here reading this book, you have the ability to achieve the specific things God has called you to do. God wants you to be specific with Him. Customize your future with great detail by being specific in prayer.

At the beginning of 2018, God took me through a season of becoming laser focused and getting rid of all distractions. During this time, the Lord spoke to me and said, "If it is not moving you forward, let it go! Let go of everything that is holding you back because you are to move forward in every area of your life." There will always be things that we must let go of in order to move forward. If you are trying to move forward but you are tied to something behind you, no matter how much you may want or try to, you will not get anywhere. You've got to get sick of things from your past trying to creep up on you. Old infirmities, habits and thoughts must go. We must move forward and take ground.

Job 17:9 says, "The righteous keep moving forward, and those with clean hands become stronger and stronger." If you are ever going to do anything great for God, you will encounter spiritual warfare. When you are under spiritual attack, you don't call in sick to your God-given destiny. You can't call up and say, "Yes, uh, hello Destiny, I can't move forward today because I'm under spiritual attack." My friends, that is not how destiny works! You have to move forward every single day.

I was writing one of my books and I physically felt horrible. I had every excuse to just take the day off and say, "I'm too sick to write today." But instead, I got a rag and laid it over my forehead, laid in bed, put on my voice dictation headset, and I continued to write. Even when you do not feel like it, keep moving forward. When you are under attack just fast, pray and push harder! Don't ever stop.

So many people give up and quit right before they were about to get their breakthrough. Don't quit on God, your dream or yourself! Every time two armies go into battle, each is trying to gain ground. In every battle there are casualties, hardships and some type of loss, but the victor always gains ground. Every time you hit a roadblock there is something to gain just on the other side. I've never gone through a hard situation and come out on the other side without gaining something.

There are no quitters in the Kingdom of God. Jesus did not quit. He carried His cross up hills, through the entire city and kept going even when the people were beating and mocking Him. He kept moving forward. The apostle Paul didn't quit either. He was thrown in jail and suffered afflictions, but he never quit. When a viper came out of the fire and bit his hand, he just shook it off. Paul let nothing stop him. He kept moving forward.

Isaiah 43:18 says, "Forget what happened in the past, and do not dwell on events from long ago." Don't hold something that your spouse did in a previous season against them. Don't make the new church you are in pay for what the last church did to you. Don't make your new employer pay for what your last employer may have done to you. Let go and move forward! If you're holding on to your past it will hold you back.

Philippians 3:13 says, "I don't depend on my own strength to accomplish this, however I do have one compelling focus: I forget all the past, as I fasten my heart toward the future!" You are not your past. Forget the past! You are everything that God says you are and who He has said you are going to be. You are a lion or lioness and you are going to roar for the Kingdom of God. Your voice is about to be heard!

Go towards everything God has placed in your heart! Many people constantly talk about the past because they are afraid to talk about the future. Fear of the future will keep you stuck in the past. We must be people who look forward to the future because we must move forward.

Your situation, whatever situation that you are in right now, isn't your future. The circumstances that you are going through right now is not your future. God has a future for you and that future is not in your past. Your past is not your future. Let me tell you what your future is. Your future is the prophetic words that God has spoken over your life. That is your future. I don't care what the devil has told you. I don't care what circumstances have come against you. I don't care what situation has convinced you that it won't happen. That is not your future.

Don't let your past keep you from moving forward into your God-given dreams and goals. Don't quit! Don't even think about quitting. One of the most helpful things you can do to move forward is to completely remove the word quit out of your dictionary. You may be looking at the natural right now in your life and saying, "There is no way that my life can line up with the prophetic words that God has spoken over my life." You know who else said that? Moses.

In Exodus 4:10, Moses argued with the Lord about why he could not do what God was saying he could do. Moses told the Lord that he stuttered and wasn't good with words. He basically said, "Forget it God. There's no way I can do what You're calling me to do." And you know what God said to Moses? God told him, "Yes, Moses, you can do it. Now go! I will be with you as you speak, and I will tell you what to say." What God was asking Moses to do was impossible in the natural. It may have been impossible for man, but it wasn't for God. Nothing is impossible with God!

You need to go back through your prayer journals, your prophetic journals, and go back and listen to all of the prophetic words that you have received from the Lord and start believing them! God will do everything that He has promised you He will do. It doesn't matter if it looks impossible! Your current situation is not your future and your past is not your future. Move forward with the prophetic words that God spoken over you!

I really believe that God wants to completely remove fear from people's hearts and lives. Do not give in to fear! Exodus 14:13 says, "And Moses said to the people, "Fear not, stand firm, and see the salvation of the Lord, which He will accomplish for you today. For the Egyptians whom you see today, you shall never see again." What if I told you that what has been chasing you won't be able to follow you where you're going? God is ready to drive out every fear you have been facing and completely get rid of your past. The things that have held you back before will never come back again. As you keep moving forward, the things behind you get further and further away. If you just bear down, set your face like a flint and keep moving forward, you will outrun your past!

The only reason the Israelites were crossing the Red Sea was to escape their past and the things that were chasing them from their past. There are so many people who are halfway through their Red Sea. It's a dangerous place to be. If you turn to the right, you will drown. If you turn to the left, the entire Red Sea is ready to crash down on you. If you turn back, things from your past will overtake you. The only choice you have is to move forward. Sometimes it's hard and sometimes it's scary but you have got to keep moving forward. Keep moving forward and you will cross over to the other side of whatever you are facing. You'll arrive on the other side, not only victorious, but totally free!

Exodus 14:14-15 says, "The Lord will fight for you when you learn to be still." The Lord said to Moses, "Why do you cry out to Me? Tell the Israelites to move on." I know none of you are like Moses. I'm sure you never give excuses about moving forward. Moses gave the Lord many excuses about why he could not move forward. He saw the Red Sea in front of them and hundreds of Egyptians chasing after them. But, in spite of all the natural obstacles, God's instruction to him was still, "Move forward!" Excuses about your past and fearing what may be ahead will keep you trapped. You must make up your mind to move forward.

I was ministering at a men's conference one time and a man came up for prayer for healing. He was physically healed right there at the altar and started crying. I could tell he was really being touched by the Lord. The next day in service, the man stood up and repented in front of the entire church. The man confessed that he had put his wife through many difficult years of marriage because of something his first wife did to him. He was only married to his first wife for 18 months and had been married to his current wife for almost 30 years! The next time I saw this man and his wife, they looked like newlyweds! They were both so happy and full of love for each other because this man finally decided to let go of his past. Don't let something from your past keep you from moving forward toward your God-ordained future.

Isaiah 43:18 says, "Forget what happened in the past and do not dwell on the events from long ago because you have a future." You must forget about what happened in the past and move forward. Your future is waiting on you!

My wife, Autumn Dawson, says something all the time and it is so true and so powerful. She says, "Regret is an invitation from your past to rob you of your future." Don't let the things in your past rob you of your future! Do not turn back, do not turn to the right or to the left, and do not look at the Egyptians who represent the things trying to chase you down from your past. Just keep moving forward. This is your time!

CHAPTER 2: WHEN IT DOESN'T MAKE SENSE

The Lord has a dream and destiny that He has placed deep inside each one of us. God put that dream inside you because God needs it manifested on Earth. Many times, what God is asking us to move forward into will not make sense. I would even dare to say that if what God is asking you to do makes sense, it's not from God. If what God is asking you to do is easy, it's not from God. If you can understand it, it's not from God because God is always calling us out into the impossible. Your destiny will look different than you thought it would so stop trying to figure it out. Trust the process that God has you on! Enjoy the journey! Move forward even when it doesn't make any sense in the natural.

I was up late one night spending some time with the Lord. As I was praying, I kept hearing one word over and over again in my spirit. That word was "yes". Then I felt the Lord say, "I want My children to have a yes in their spirit, in their heart, in their mind, in their mouth and in their actions."

As I heard this "yes" continue to echo through my spirit, I was reminded of something my wife, Autumn, prophesied about 3 weeks before this. Autumn said this: "God wants you to say yes to your next season before you know what it is." If God can get your yes, even before it all makes sense, then He knows He can trust you with the big things He wants to do through you. Almost every time God has asked my wife and I to step out and start something new, we haven't had the resources, team, finances, talent or ability to complete it. But we have always said yes anyways. We said yes even before we knew all the specifics of how God was going to accomplish it. But when God had our yes, He came through every single time!

The first thing you have to know about your yes is that there are unbelievable things on the other side of it. Your yes to moving forward will always cost you something, but every yes to God has a powerful reward. Many times, God will draw you closer to Himself before He reveals His plan or His next step for you. God wants our yes to moving forward before we know what we're moving forward into. When God fully has your yes, He will open doors for you that only He can. When you surrender to whatever God is asking you to say yes to, the Lord will begin to do impossible things through you.

Saying yes to God can correct years of mistakes. Many people make mistakes and miss out on their destiny because of fear of stepping out. They don't move forward because they don't believe what God has said about them and about their purpose. Mistakes in life come from saying no to God, but if you will give God one yes, He can undo all of your mistakes and move you forward.

One of the things I love most about God is that every single day we have a chance to start over. Every day is another chance to move forward. When my son, Ezra, was 4, he started playing t-ball. Ever since Ezra was very small, I have taken him out for "man adventures" so that we can spend time together. One week, I told Ezra I wanted to take him out for one of our "man adventures". He was enjoying his time with his mom, my beautiful wife, Autumn, and hesitated when I told him it was time for us to go. I knew he would love what I had planned for him but didn't want to ruin the surprise. Instead of telling him everything I had planned for us to do, I told him, "Ezra, I'll give you a hint. There will be ice cream." He was immediately excited and shouted, "Yes!" Isn't that just like our relationship with Father God? God wants our yes before we know exactly what He has for us. He wants our yes even when it doesn't make sense yet because everything He wants us to say yes to is going to be amazing!

When we give God our yes, even when it doesn't make sense, amazing things begin to happen. Freedom floods our lives and the Kingdom of God starts to manifest everywhere around us. There is restoration inside of your yes. God will use your yes to correct years of mistakes. Your yes unleashes God's power in your life and in the lives of every single person in your realm of influence. Remember, God has unbelievable things waiting in store for you on the other side of your yes!

God will ask you to do things that seem like the craziest thing you've ever heard of. It won't always make sense in the natural, and you may not have enough money in the bank to achieve it, but if you say "yes," God will make a way. So many people are waiting for the provision to show up before they will step out to pursue their dreams. We want God to bring us the provision before we step out. But God always calls us to step out before He manifests the provision. This is just like in James 4:8, "Draw near to

God and He will draw near to you." We have to step out first and when God sees our yes, He always brings the resources and people we need to make our God-given dreams a reality. One person saying "yes" to God can change everything.

My wife, Autumn, and I were praying for a financial breakthrough for our ministry. There were several specific resources we needed the finances for in order to move forward. I was in corporate prayer one evening and I heard the word "SUPPLIES". Then I heard the Lord say, "I am the Great Supplier. Run after Me and your calling like you already have all your supplies, because you already do." My friends, I became extremely excited when the Lord spoke these words to me.

Whenever the Lord speaks to you and says, "I AM," whatever He says after those words is exactly what He is about to become in your life. If we understood that God has all the supplies that we need to fulfill every single prophecy spoken over our lives, we would move forward without worrying about it making sense. We can trust God to give us everything we need, when we need it. That is exactly what Matthew 6:33 promises, ""But seek first the Kingdom of God and His righteousness, and all these things will be added to you." When we seek God's Kingdom first, knowing He is the Great Supplier, He will make sure we always have everything we need to move forward.

God impressed on my spirit so strongly that He is ready to release His supplies to many people so that they can fulfill the calling upon their life. As the Lord was speaking this to me, I had a vision of crates full of supplies that people need to fulfill their destiny. As I saw these crates, I heard the words "careful" and "crates full." As I prayed, I heard the Lord say, "There are people who are always careful about everything but they will never get the crates full of supplies that I have for them." If you are careful and worried about where the provision for your vision is going to come from, you will miss out on the crates full of supplies God wants to give you.

Philippians 4:6-7 says, "Be careful for nothing; but in everything, by prayer and supplication with thanksgiving, let your requests be made known unto God. And the peace of God, which passes all understanding, shall keep your hearts and minds through Christ Jesus." If you play it safe and worry about everything making sense first, you won't move forward. But God is looking for those that will step out in adventurous faith and depend on Him to supply everything. With God as our Great Supplier, we do not have to worry about how everything will work out or when God will bring specific supplies into our lives. God is faithful to always bring the right resources, people and finances to us exactly when we need them.

Philippians 4:19 says, "And my God shall supply all your need according to His riches in glory by Christ Jesus." For too long we have looked to the right and to the left to try to get man's provision for the vision God has given us, but it is time for you to move forward! No man can supply all of the needs for what God wants to do in and through you. This is the hour that God wants us to look to Him as the Great Supplier to receive the supplies we need from

Heaven. God will give us more than enough to complete all that He has in store for us. He is the Great Supplier!

God has proven this to my wife, Autumn, and I over and over again. One time, we needed a specific amount of money in order to do something. My wife estimated how much we would need and just said a specific number. Just a few days later, someone handed us a check for that exact amount of money. Whenever you want to do something, God will provide for it. You don't have to worry about it. God will take care of you. Matthew 6:27 says, "Can any one of you by worrying add a single hour to your life?" Worry will rob you of time. When you worry, you are just wasting time. There were seasons of my life where I worried about certain things all the time. As long as I was worrying about those things, they never got better. But as soon as I quit worrying, God worked it all out.

The longer I walk with the Lord, the more I encounter hard seasons. But I always learn so much from those tough seasons. Hard seasons can be hard to understand. Difficult things come into our lives and many times they don't make any sense. Try as you may, it may be extremely difficult to understand why it's all happening. But the next time you are going through a hard time, just remind yourself that God has promised to work every single bit of it out for your good. Romans 8:28 says, "We know that all things work together for the good of those who love God: those who are called according to His purpose." Whenever you come upon another difficult situation, just believe and know that God is going to work it out for your good. Choose to have faith and give glory to God for the good outcome of your situation in advance.

I am who I am today because of the hard seasons I've walked through. When spiritual fathers and mentors have stabbed me in the back, I thank them for it. When spiritual sons and daughters walk away from me, I thank them for it. When I was let go from one position or another, I was thankful for it because the hard times are what pushed me into my destiny. Even when everything that is going on doesn't make any sense, we must keep moving forward. When you are going through something, keep going! That's the only way you'll get through it and to the other side.

When what we are going through doesn't make sense we must simply trust the Lord. Proverbs 3:5-6 says, "Trust in the Lord with all your heart, and do not lean on your own understanding. In all your ways acknowledge Him, and He will make your paths straight." When we are following God, there is nothing we can lean on except for Him. We must lean on what the Lord has said. What God is doing in our lives will not make sense in to our natural understanding. Whenever God gives me a word or a promise about something, I write it down and keep it visible in front of me. I keep it ever before me because many times the natural will look the opposite of what God has said.

In 2 Chronicles 20, Jehoshaphat was leading the children of Israel into battle against the Ammonites and Moabites. The Bible goes on to say that reports came back to Jehoshaphat that the other armies were all about to come against them and they were outnumbered. Verse 3 says, "And Jehoshaphat feared, and set himself to seek the Lord, and proclaimed a fast throughout all Judah." This was Jehoshaphat's strategy to move forward. Jehoshaphat did not go to all his men and say, "Hurry guys! We need to do some push-ups and get the blacksmiths to forge us some powerful weapons." Instead, Jehoshaphat called a fast to seek the Lord because he knew the battle was not his, but the Lord's. Jehoshaphat chose to move forward spiritually instead of in the natural. What God was telling Jehoshaphat to do made no sense. But Jehoshaphat moved forward anyway.

Sometimes spending 15 hours on a project is productive. But sometimes setting aside 2 days and getting away on a prayer retreat is more productive. We have to be led by the Holy Spirit on what strategy to use to move forward. It will be different in every season. In what ways are you choosing to move forward in this season?

Jehoshaphat knew that, at this time, prayer was his most effective strategy to move forward. In 2 Chronicle 20:12 Jehoshaphat prayed, "O our God, will You not judge them? For we have no power against this great multitude that is coming against us; nor do we know what to do, but our eyes are upon You." What Jehoshaphat was saying was, "God, without You, I can't win this." The spiritual attacks that come against you and the things you go through in life, you can't do it, unless you fast and pray. With God you will have a complete victory. When we realize that without God we can't win, we will win with Him fighting our battles every time.

God replied to Jehoshaphat in 2 Chronicles 20:15-17

and said, "Do not be afraid nor dismayed because of this great multitude, for the battle is not yours, but God's. You will not need to fight in this battle. Position yourselves, stand still and see the salvation of the Lord, who is with you, O Judah and Jerusalem!" This was all the reassurance Jehoshaphat needed. The next day all the men in the army showed up with all their battle gear on and Jehoshaphat said, "Not needed; I've got a word from God."

You can imagine how ridiculous the men must have thought this was. There were three armies coming against them. These armies were bigger than the Israelite army and wanted to destroy them. Jehoshaphat told them that they didn't need their armor or weaponry to fight this battle because God would fight for them. Jehoshaphat used the strategy that the Lord had given him and picked out men to lead the army in worship. Worship! Jehoshaphat was leading his men into battle and they were going to worship their way to victory.

2 Chronicle 20:22 says, "Now when they began to sing and to praise, the Lord set ambushes against the people of Ammon, Moab, and Mount Seir, who had come against Judah; and they were defeated." You see what happened was two of the armies paired up to go against the third army. Then after the first two armies defeated the third army, they started to gather the spoils. But then the two armies starting fighting over the spoils. Then the next thing you know, all of the men from the three armies, that were coming against Jehoshaphat and the Israelite army, had all killed each other off!

2 Chronicles 20:24 says, "So when Judah came to a place overlooking the wilderness, they looked toward the multitude; and there were their dead bodies, fallen on the earth. No one had escaped." So, Jehoshaphat and his men went and gathered all of the spoil from the other three armies without ever lifting a sword! The Bible even says there was so much treasure and livestock and spoil that they couldn't even carry it all! They spent three days gathering it all into the Israelite camp.

God came through for them just like He told Jehoshaphat He would. Jehoshaphat followed the strategy of the Lord to move forward and God fought His battle for him. Just remember, my friends, you've got to know how God wants you to move forward because it will be different in every season. And know that when you're going through something, you're gaining ground.

This was a season where Jehoshaphat said, "There is nothing I can do in the flesh to defeat these armies that are coming against me, but I am going to fast, pray and worship God." Because of this, they got the victory. No matter how impossible your situation looks, God will send you back from the battle with so much of the spoils that you won't even be able to handle it all!

I was walking through some hard circumstances one time and the Lord woke me up very early one morning. As soon as I woke up, I heard these words "Keep going, keep going, keep going, keep going" numerous times. So I jumped out of bed and headed to the prayer room. On my way, I heard these words "Keep moving, keep moving, keep moving, keep moving." So I kept moving.

When I got into the prayer room I heard the Lord say this, "Tell my children to keep moving forward." Then I felt impressed to look up Matthew 4:23. It says, "And Jesus went about all of Galilee, teaching in the synagogues, preaching the gospel of the kingdom, and healing all kinds of sickness and all kinds of disease amongst the people." In this passage we see that Jesus was always moving and moving forward. He always kept going, doing the will of the Father. No matter what, Jesus always kept going.

We see in the life of Jesus that there are many times that He did numerous signs, wonders and miracles and the people rejoiced. We also see numerous times when many people came against Him. But none of these things moved Him. Jesus was steadfast in His mission and constantly in prayer. This is where He maintained the strength to keep moving forward to do everything He saw God, the Father, doing.

In prayer, I felt the Lord impress upon me strongly to tell people who may think that their life really doesn't matter or that what they're doing for God is very insignificant that, "If you could see God's greater plan, even years down the road, you would see that He is molding and shaping you to do something very powerful for Him." I challenge you to not allow the current situations of what you see in the natural make you shrink back. Instead, let them become like fuel to move you forward. Move forward confidently in the things of the Lord.

In Genesis 12, we find the story of Abraham. He was

a young man at this time, he was 75 and he was about to inherit everything from his father. He had stayed with his father for all these years and just when he was about to get his inheritance, the Lord spoke to him. Genesis 12:1-3 says, "Now the Lord had said to Abram: "Get out of your country, from your family and from your father's house, to a land that I will show you." God was asking Abraham to give up everything he had worked for, all of his inheritance for an unknown land that God wouldn't even tell him where it was! This made no sense. Even though it didn't make sense to Abraham, he did what the Lord told him to do. Verse 3 says, "So Abram departed as the Lord had spoken to him, and Lot went with him. And Abram was seventy-five years old when he departed from Haran." The Lord made this promise to Abraham, "I will make you a great nation; I will bless you and make your name great; and you shall be a blessing." How could God make him a great nation if he had no children? How was the Lord going to make Abraham's name great, if he had no children who carried his name?

The promise didn't make sense, and even though Abraham didn't receive the promise until 24 years later, Abraham still believed the promise. In his waiting, Abraham produced Ishmael because he got tired of waiting. Abraham may have been tired of waiting but in his impatience his produced Ishmael, but Isaac was on the way! Some of you have been waiting for so long that you are in danger of producing an Ishmael. You may be saying, "God it has been too long. I've waited all this time and still haven't gotten my breakthrough. Nothing has come through yet. What in the world is going on? I'm just going to have to push through and make it happen." You see, what happens is when we are waiting on our promise, and it seems to be delayed, we get frustrated. But the thing is, the promise from God is a supernatural promise, and in our frustration, we attach natural reasons why it is not happening.

How many times do we get frustrated while we're waiting and blame a person or a circumstance? But Ephesians 6:12 tells us that, "We do not wrestle against flesh and blood, but against principalities and powers." We're not fighting things in the natural, we're fighting things in the spiritual realm. But rest assured knowing that what God has promised you is more important to God than it is to you. So don't worry; God will bring it to pass! We just need to let Him guide us. We need to surrender fully to Him and trust His wisdom so we do not step out of His will. Don't produce an Ishmael when Isaac is on the way!

Abraham had to leave everything that made him comfortable. He had to leave his father's wealth, his own house, and the land that he was about to inherit. The gardens were already planted and the cattle were already raised. Everything in the natural looked good right where he was. But the promise wasn't going to come from where he was comfortable. The promise was where God was calling him to go, outside of his comfort zone. God will call you outside of your comfort zone and it may not make sense, but there are so many other promises wrapped up in your saying, "yes" to your promise!

CHAPTER 3: DON'T BELIEVE THE LIE

Galatians 5:7-9 says, "You ran well. Who hindered you from obeying the truth? This persuasion does not come from Him who calls you. A little leaven leavens the whole lump." The first thing the enemy does, when we receive a word from God, is to try to hinder us by bringing doubt, fear or worry to whatever God has said.

In another translation, Galatians 5:7-9 says this, "Before you were led astray you were so faithful to Jesus. Why have you turned away from what is right and true? Who deceived you? The one who enfolded you into His grace isn't behind this false teaching you have believed. Not at all! Do you know when you believe a little lie it can change your complete belief system."

When you've stopped moving forward, you need to ask yourself who deceived you? You need to ask the Holy Spirit, "Holy Spirit, who deceived me? When was I deceived and what is the truth?" God loves you so much that He will tell you what lie you've believed, who deceived you, and what the truth is. Then you can go back, repent from that, and start back from where you were.

There are times when I've done counseling and I've encountered 30, 40 and even 50 year-old individuals, that in some areas, act like they are 13. Why is that? Almost every time, when we would finally get to the root of the issues, we could track back to something that went wrong when they were 13. Many times, people will walk around believing a lie the enemy sowed into their minds decades ago. Don't let those lies hold you back and keep you from moving forward. Be willing to do some self-examination, as the Holy Spirit leads you, so that you can be set free from those lies.

How many people do you know, who were once so faithful to the Lord at one time, but now...what happened? Believing one lie can totally take you out. All children believe that they can do anything. Children believe anything is possible until someone or something tells them that they can't or they aren't. So many times in our life, we have been deceived about who we are and what we can do. I have some nicknames that I call my son to let him know how much I believe in him. One day, my son, Ezra came in and said, "Dad, if anybody ever tells me I'm not that or I can't do that, I'm going to tell them that's not true because you said I am and that I can!" I was amazed! A father's voice is so powerful.

For some of you, all you need to move forward is to hear what the Father says about you. Ask the Father who He says you are. I'm telling you, my friends, there is nothing more powerful to move you forward than the approval of your Heavenly Father. When you know who you are in God, it won't matter what anyone else says.

People will always be critical when someone tries to bring about change. Jesus stepped on the scene and had many people coming against Him. They were criticizing Him because everywhere He went, He brought change. When you are running hard after God and your destiny, you will have critics. But don't worry about them. They are only complaining because you are running and they are standing still. All of the movement you are creating is frustrating them, but don't worry.

Dead criticism cannot attach to a moving vessel. People who are not moving forward are often critical of those who are. As you keep moving forward, you will pass them and eventually their voices will fade away because they are not going where you are going. Keep moving forward and you'll outrun your critics.

Autumn and I went and saw an awesome movie on a date night one time. It was "The Greatest Showman". This is still one of our favorite movies today. In the movie, the main character, P.T. Barnum, is talking to his wife about their critics. The wife replies by telling him, "Society will never accept us, because if they did, they would have to stop talking about us and do something with their lives." Critics are critical! It's just who they are, but don't listen to them. Let the voice of God be the loudest voice in your life.

When the Kingdom of God fully comes into your life even the unbeliever will notice. Even those who have come against you in the past will understand that the Kingdom of God has completely manifested in your life. You will not have to announce the blessings and favor of God that is on your life; everyone will know. Why? I'm so glad you asked. It is because the unbelievers and your critics will see the faithfulness of God through your life. That, in itself, will be a powerful witness to compel them to follow Him.

Some of you are your own worst critic. Don't be critical of yourself! God believes in you or He would not have called you. Do you think the Lord would ever say, "Hey, do you remember that one day when I called you two years ago? Uh, yeah. I'm really sorry but I made a mistake." No, my friends! Romans 11:29 says, "For the gifts and the calling of God are irrevocable." When God calls you, no matter what, His call is still there. You know what God's call is? It's an invitation where God says, "Come on, come closer to Me. Do you want this? I'll do great things through you. You've just got to walk with Me."

Proverbs 17:22 says, "A joyful heart is like good medicine." Discouragement will keep you from moving forward in all God has for you. This is why you need to encourage yourself in the Lord daily. Let the joy of the Lord constantly encourage you so you can move forward. The world needs the joy of the Lord and God wants us to take it to our workplaces, our families, our churches, and everywhere we go.

Psalm 32:8 says, "I will stay close to you, instructing and guiding you along the pathway of your life. I will advise you along the way and lead you forward with My eyes as your guide." Another translation says, "I will instruct you and teach you in the way that you should go. I will counsel you with my eye upon you." This Scripture should remove all fear and insecurity from your life, my friends! God is promising here that He will stay close to you and instruct you.

Think about it; if you get your instructions from God, you shouldn't worry about anything! Anytime you buy something that has to be put together, it comes with an instruction manual and a blueprint. If you follow those instructions properly, whatever you put together will work. If you will listen to God, He will instruct you. If you follow His instructions, then your life can, and will, function properly!

In Psalm 32:8, God goes onto to say that He will teach us as we are moving forward in the journey of life. God promises to teach us and show us the way, so we don't have to worry. God is with us and is guiding us as we move forward. He's watching over us every step of the way. So this means that God is going to help you with that new business you want to start. God is going to help you with that new ministry you are thinking of launching. Newly married couples, it's going to be ok! God is going to see you and your spouse through whatever you're going through. You may have just had your first child. You're going to be ok. God is going to help you!

God also promises that He will counsel us. People go to counseling for many different reasons. You can go to counseling if you need to get over past hurts, improve relationships, figure out why you may be stuck in a certain area or for so many other different reasons. But this Scripture is saying that God will be our counselor. Many times in counseling, you will speak with someone in confidence. You bare your heart and soul freely and openly to them and then allow them to speak into your life. This is what God is saying He wants to do for you. He will counsel you.

And then, finally, in the last part of Psalm 32:8, God says, "My eyes are upon you." What better feeling could we possibly have than knowing that God, our loving

Father, is looking at us with favor? As you move forward, move forward with confidence. God is looking upon you. He is going to show you the way to go and He is going to instruct you in what to do. What do you have to fear or worry about? God's got you! He is in full control and He is making a way before you, so you can move forward. Allow Him to guide you, lead you and move you forward!

CHAPTER 4: FORWARD VISION (Autumn Dawson)

The nature of those who walk in the apostolic is to move forward. It pushes the gifts and assignments in others to move and advance in their own lives as well. In my own life, I have experienced times where I wanted to move forward with things in my life and calling but felt opposition, fear, or even as if I was in a fog. Fog by definition is a thick cloud of water droplets in the atmosphere that obscures or restricts visibility. For me, if I don't have a clear view of where I am supposed to move or go, I tend to hesitate to move forward. That hesitation can cause detours and delays in your life and calling. The most successful people in the Kingdom of God are very clear on what they are believing for. They pursue the purpose on their lives and are driven towards people and situations that will further their Kingdom assignments. When things are foggy, they stir things up and push past the opposition and fear.

I am reminded of a time when playing Super Mario Brothers with my son, it's one of his favorite games. There is a level on the game where a cloud blows smoke or fog at the players to keep them from seeing the right path to take. The result can be that Mario falls in a hole and loses a life, takes the wrong way, or worse, gets scorched by a fire breathing plant. However, if you get in the fog and begin to shake around, the fog clears, and you can see where to go. As we move forward with our lives, sometimes we must shake ourselves from complacency and fear, and go take down the fire breathing enemies trying to destroy us. It didn't take me very long to realize in the game that I was tired of dodging the plant's fireballs. If I conquered the plant, then I wouldn't have to keep dodging it. We need to stop dodging the things that are defeating us. When you can't see the whole picture, just begin to shake whatever is obstructing your view and take the first step.

Let's talk about a few ways to move forward in your life. The first way is to defeat complacency. You defeat complacency by pushing yourself past yourself. I once heard that if you are the smartest person in the room, you are in the wrong room. We must find people in life that will push us and hold us accountable to what we are called to do. Have you ever had an idea or thought and decided you didn't want to tell anyone, because they would pester you until you followed through with it. Me too! I'm actually married to a person who wouldn't leave me alone until I did it. I would often shy away from sharing my thoughts and dreams with others, saying I was using wisdom by just praying about it. But really, I was actually just complacent and afraid. I already knew what God was calling me to do. I also knew It was going to require effort, lots of faith and cause me to break up with complacency.

Another way to move forward with your life is to get clear on where you are going. I was very vague in what I was moving towards in my life, so I was getting very vague results. In my mind, I always thought I would someday do this or someday have that. Let's face it, someday was never coming. I needed vision to move forward. The Bible says in Habakkuk 2:3 to write what you see. Write it in big block letters, so that it can be read on the run. The vision message is a witness pointing to what's coming. There is an accountability attached to writing down where you are headed. When you see it in black and white, it is no longer vague or abstract.

I remember the day I wrote down vision for my life and the direction I was headed towards. I wanted to hide it in my notebook. However, the scripture says to write it in big block letters so that others can see it. I wrote my vision down and taped it up in our closet. My husband, Joe was on a ministry trip. I just knew when he got home, he would have some questions about it and begin to help me get there. He got in late that night, so the next day he began asking what was hanging in our closet. I replied just like the scripture said, "This is the vision pointing to where my life is heading." Like I anticipated, Joe was very driven about holding me accountable to the vision. You see, I think God was very intentional when He inspired Habakkuk to write about vision. He was clear, "Write it down (don't be vague). Make it plain and bold (don't complicate it), and let others see it (have accountability), so they will know where you are headed." Getting clear vision for your life and sharing it with those you trust is a strategy out of complacency. This is forward thinking and forward moving.

Accountability is a strategy to moving forward. The Lord spoke to me about making a big decision I had been praying about for over a year. I remember the first thing I did, I told three trusted friends. We were at a restaurant, after a worship service. We sat down after ordering and I blurted out, "The Lord spoke to me and I am quitting my job." They all just looked at each other and probably were shocked at my direct statement. I told them because I needed accountability about what I heard from God. I told them because I knew they would pray for me. I told them because I needed to give voice to what God had spoken to me. My trustworthy friends are the ones who would stand with me when I had to write my notice and when I had to pack up my office. They were the ones who would stand with me when I had to answer questions that didn't make sense to people, who were not praying about my life, and had other expectations of me. You need people full of faith and vision in your corner. You need people who know where your life is headed so that they can help you stay focused.

Your life is too valuable to waste. It's never too late to get a vision or direction from God. If you want to know why you are always living in the past, it is probably because you have no vision for the future. Regret is an invitation from your past to rob you of your future. Don't accept the invite. Don't live a life of regrets. Start today like I did and get that vision on the wall. Get some accountability with trustworthy people and shake the fog off. I can tell you from experience that I have accomplished more in 3 months than I did in 3 years because I got clear on where I was going. I am moving forward because I have vision.

If you are unsure about the vision for your life, the best way to find out about your destiny is to get closer to the one who wrote it. God wrote a book about your life before you ever lived the first day. Psalm 139:16 says, "You saw me before I was born, every day of my life was recorded in your books. Every moment was laid out before a single day passed." You cannot move forward until you know where you are headed. There is a beautiful life out there waiting for you to pursue it and there are people waiting for you to step into your purpose.

Isaiah 43:16-18 says, "This is what God says, the God who builds a road right through the middle of the ocean, who carves a path through pounding waves, The God who summons horses and chariots and armies. Forget about what's happened; don't keep going over old history. Be alert, be present. I'm about to do something brand new." I love this portion of scripture. Quit going over old history, I am about to do something brand new. Let's face it, our old history can cause us to be discouraged and leave us doubtful. There is something wonderful about a new start. I think about the start of a new school year and how the first day sets a whole new rhythm for our house. Everyone is in bed early, they know what they are wearing the next day, they have a new schedule for their lives. My teenage daughter, who I could barely peel out of bed over the Summer, suddenly wants to get up early and fix her hair and makeup. This is simply because she knows where she is going. God wants to give you a brand-new start and move you forward with vision. Vision will do that for a person, it will drive them to push past complacency and discomfort to accomplish things they would never do without it.

Prophets and prophetic people have prophetic vision. They will often see what a situation or person is supposed to look like. Then they will prophesy, declare and decree over that person or situation what they are seeing. The responsibility of the word then falls on the one who received the word. If you don't put action behind the prophecy, vision or declaration, you will remain in your comfort zone, in a stagnant place or worse, you will stay the same. Can you imagine your life if it never moved forward? What if you stayed in the same place year after year? You were created to grow and advance. The Bible says that we go from glory to glory. I believe we achieve this by going from yes to yes. When God asks you to step out or to advance, what is your natural tendency? Is it hesitation? I have found the more I hesitate to say yes to God, the more stagnant I become in my life. Instead of yes to yes, I began to say from how to how.

I have seen this happen over and over in the lives of believers. They get a prophetic word or have a prophetic dream or vision and do nothing with it. They are stuck in the same place spiritually and naturally and want to blame others who were willing to put in the effort to move forward. It reminds me of the scripture in James that says, "Faith without works is dead", in fact I don't think its faith at all. The difference between visionaries and people of complacency is this, visionaries are always stretching themselves. They are willing to confront awkward and uncomfortable situations in order to move forward. They continually push themselves outside of their comfort zone in order to avoid complacency. Complacency is the enemy of creative thinkers, they avoid it by deliberately doing things out of the box. Visionaries are always moving forward, they see what's out in front of them, and plan their time, energy and resources to get what they see.

Your mindset could be one of the biggest roadblocks to moving forward. In my study of the mind and mindset, I discovered some things biologically that I didn't realize. Our mind is a huge memory bank. It stores information and content over years. We store major amounts of information by the time we enter adulthood, as much as one hundred times what the encyclopedia has listed in it. That's a lot of information! All our habits, ways of thinking, and actions are all collected in the part of our mind called the subconscious. Your subconscious works hard to keep you in your comfort zone. If you think about doing something different from what you have stored in your subconscious, you all of the sudden get tensed up, uneasy or maybe even sweat! What I have learned is that if I want to grow and move forward, I must remember the scripture in Isaiah that says, "Forget about the past, I am doing something new." Some of us need to reprogram our thinking. See, your mind has kept you in your comfort zone but it's also kept you out of your destiny. Just visualize yourself taking a bigger step and doing some new things.

I recently had a vision of many people running a race and a roadblock was set up in the path of the course. A road block is a structure that is set up to keep you from moving forward on the path. Usually when there is a roadblock, they will tell you to take an alternate route or a detour. In the vision, the mind was the roadblock. It was telling you that you can't go that way, it will take you out of your comfort zone, it will cause you to be stretched and take you to new places. The vision challenged me greatly! Stop looking for alternate routes and detours to your destiny. When a mindset shows up that says you can't do what God has said you can, you have to decide, am I going to believe this or push past the roadblock? The enemy will always throw up a smokescreen to the truth. He will always paint a picture of the worst when God has already provided a path to move forward into the best. When you encounter opposition, distractions or resistance from the enemy in your life, simply do this, take authority and move on. Moving on will move you forward, quit going over old history or the past. Move On! What happened before is not what God has planned for your next. Change your past memories into hopeful expectations of what God can and will do for you.

Hebrews 12:2 says, "Fix our eyes on Jesus who began and finished His race." He never lost sight of where He was headed. He endured the cross because of the joy that was set before Him. Jesus knew His purpose. He had a vision for what the end would look like. Luke 4:43 says, "I must preach the Kingdom of God, for this is the reason I have been sent." What is the reason you were sent? It's time to move forward with that reason. You have everything you need to move forward. All the resources of Heaven are brought to you by Holy Spirit.

CHAPTER 5: WHO'S BEHIND YOU?

Joshua 1:1-2 says, "After the death of Moses, the servant of the Lord, it came to pass that the Lord spoke to Joshua the son of Nun, Moses' assistant, saying: "Moses, My servant, is dead. Now therefore, arise, go over this Jordan, you and all this people, to the land which I am giving to them—the children of Israel. Every place that the sole of your foot will tread upon I have given you, as I said to Moses." God comes to Joshua and tells him to move forward and accomplish something that the generation behind him did not do. There are people in previous generations who were called to do something, but they did not do it. But you can.

Generations before you have dropped mantles, callings, and assignments. People in the past may have said no to those things, but because those things were spoken into existence by the Lord, they are still out there to be completed by the next generation. Some of you, all you have to do is lean down and pick up something that one of your ancestors laid down. Some of your parents or grandparents were called to be ministers or entrepreneurs but they were scared to step out and do it. You can take on that same anointing and pick up what they laid down and do something great for God.

In Joshua 1:5-9, the Lord encourages Joshua four times to be strong and courageous. In verse 5, He tells Joshua, "No man shall be able to stand before you all the days of your life; as I was with Moses, so I will be with you. I will not leave you nor forsake you." Then, in verse 6, the Lord tells Joshua, "Be strong and of good courage, for to this people you shall divide as an inheritance the land which I swore to their fathers to give them." Then, a third time, God says to Joshua, "Only be strong and very courageous, that you may observe to do according to all the law which Moses, My servant, commanded you." And, finally, God encourages Joshua one more time, "Have I not commanded you? Be strong and of good courage; do not be afraid, nor be dismayed, for the Lord your God is with you wherever you go."

God was giving Joshua instructions and encouragement because God wanted Joshua to move forward with what Moses had not been able to accomplish. We must move forward with whatever God has assigned us to do. The reason God called you to do something is because God needs it done in the Earth. I don't care if God has called you to own a nail salon or a car dealership. Whatever it is that God has called you to do, do it! He gave it to you for a reason. If you do not do it, you will watch someone else do it.

God told Joshua to move forward in the natural and take a multitude of others with him. How many people are behind you waiting for you to act on the word God has given you? What if, when you step out, whatever you are doing explodes and you are in a position to employ 100 people? You just made 100 families better. What if you stepped out in ministry and thousands of people's lives are changed by God? What if?

You have no idea how many people may follow you after you move forward. Just like with God's commandment to Joshua, whatever God has called you to do, there are hundreds of people depending on you to obey and follow through. There are many waiting on you to do what God has called you to do. Other people's destinies are locked up inside of your commitment to move forward.

One Sunday at our church, ROAR Church, in Texarkana, Texas, I told our people, "I'm about to run around this church. We're about to get a breakthrough." I took off running thinking I would probably be the only one to run around. Then I looked behind me and there were probably 20 people running behind me! When you step out, and start to run and move forward, you may think you're the only one that's going to be running, but think of who's coming behind you? How many people are waiting for you to just start running so they can run too?

Isaiah 43:19 says, "Behold, I will do a new thing. Now it shall spring forth. Shall you not know it? I will even make a road in the wilderness and rivers in the desert." A road in the wilderness? A river in the desert? That sounds almost impossible. That's why God needs pioneers. The word pioneer means "to open and prepare the way for others to follow." This is why apostles love Isaiah 43:19. We make a path where there is no path and bring water to dry places. Most apostolic works start in very dry regions.

Pioneers keep moving ahead, they hear from Heaven and continually keep the current of what Heaven is saying flowing. Pioneers will fight whatever stands in front of their progress. God wants you to move forward, make a road in the wilderness and become a pioneer. The pioneers of old were people who went out and settled in lands that had not yet been developed. God is not going to build a road for the next generation. He has called you to partner with Him to build a road for those that will come after you! He's calling you to make a road in the wilderness and go where no one has gone before. If you don't keep moving forward, those that are behind you have nowhere to go!

Pioneers made a way where there wasn't one before so that people could come behind them and live in that new territory. We are pioneers, my friends, and pioneers always keep moving forward! In every hard time, every time you hit a roadblock or come up against a mountain, remember that the call on your life is bigger than you. God is using you to make a path for others. God will give you strength to press forward, in spite of everything that comes against you, to make a road and a path in the wilderness for those coming behind to follow. Your children, both natural and spiritual, will not have to go through the same things you went through if you keep moving forward.

Isaiah goes on to say, in the last part of this verse, "I will make rivers in the desert." Think about what a desert is like for a moment. It's dry, it's hot and there is no water. People in the desert are dehydrated and thirsty. They're tired and starving. A river in the desert is there to bring refreshing to people. You are a river in the desert of this world for God. You are a prophetic pioneer. God is going to use you to make a new way so that those behind you can move forward even faster than you were able to. If you move forward every day of your life, your life will bring refreshment to so many people. You have what they need. John says, "Rivers of living water will flow the core of your being." You have what those behind you need but you've just got to allow God to bring it out.

The Lord gave me a very powerful prophetic dream about making a way for others. In the dream, I was in a long hall. Then the Lord asked me, "What do you see?" I answered and said, "Lord, I see a long hallway with a door at the end." The Lord then told me to start walking towards the door and to tell Him what I was seeing. I started walking towards the door and I noticed that the door at the end of the hallway was very beautiful. It was a white, rustic-looking door. The Lord asked me again, "What else do you see?" I answered, "I see a doorknob."

Then the Lord spoke to me so powerfully. He said, "Stare at the keyhole. You may be at the very beginning of the hall but when you get to the other end of the hall, and reach the door, if you will stare at the keyhole, you will realize that this door will not open unless you have a key that fits perfectly inside of it." Then I felt the Lord say this, "I want to make a remnant of people the key. If anyone is willing to move towards this door, and focus on the keyhole, I will make them the key." Some want to focus on the hall. Others may focus on the door, or the doorknob, but very few in the remnant of God are focusing on the keyhole.

Why is the keyhole so important? The keyhole is important because if no one is the key, then no one in the hallway is getting through the door. If no one is willing to become the key then no one who is standing at the door, or reaching for the doorknob, will be able to open the door. We have many people just standing around waiting or pulling on the doorknob. But God is looking for a remnant of people who will allow Him to chisel them down to become the key to open the door for themselves and so many others. God wants you to let Him chisel you down and shape you to fit perfectly inside the keyhole to unlock things for the next generation. He wants to form you into the perfect key to unlock His unlimited resources and potential for your family, your church, your city, and your region.

Then the Lord told me something kind of funny because I'm southern and southern gentlemen open doors for people. He said, "Become the key to unlock the keyhole and open the door. Swing it wide and tell everyone to come on through and let everyone pass you by."

Remember when Joshua took the children of Israel over to the Promised Land. He told the priests to carry the arch up before the people and stand. The priests stood in the middle of the Jordan until everyone had passed them by. This is what a keyhole remnant does. They become the key to unlock the door and tell everyone to run on ahead and pass them. What do true spiritual fathers and mothers want? They want all of their sons and daughters to go past them and achieve more than they ever could for God.

I had a good friend of mine give me a prophetic word one time. He said, "Joe, the very height of your ministry is your ceiling, but your ceiling is going to be your son's floor." As far as we go in life, and however much we accomplish, our natural children are supposed to go further and do more. Our spiritual sons and daughters are supposed to go further and do more as well. In life, everything I start or build, I do it to eventually give it away. Everything we do for the Kingdom of God is not just about us moving forward, it's about those who are coming behind us.

CHAPTER 6: NEXT LEVEL FRIENDS

Who you are running with determines how you move forward! God has specific people He wants to place in your life to help move you forward. God gives us strategic relationships to bring forth the purposes of the Kingdom. But the enemy also has people he wants to plant in your life to derail your purpose. The enemy's number one strategy against you is to get you to run with the wrong people. We must have great discernment in our relationships. Many times good relationships and bad relationships are not as easy to discern as we would think.

One time, I had an open ministry date and a minister that I really admire called me and asked if he could come through and speak at our ministry on that exact date. I wanted to immediately say, "yes" but I heard the Holy Spirit tell me no. I politely declined the offer and he asked me, "Who is speaking that night?" I was just honest with him and told him that the Holy Spirit told me no. He thanked me for being obedient to the Lord and that was the end of the conversation.

Then the Lord spoke to me about bringing in a different minister. This minister was someone I was not fully confident in. The Lord spoke to me and said, "Maybe this is for this minister and not really about the people. I want you to create this opportunity for this person." I told the Lord, "But God, I don't really think that way." The Lord spoke to me and said, "I know you don't, but I do."

In order to move forward, we must obey the voice of the Lord in our relationships. We don't always think about people the way the Lord does but we must start thinking the way God thinks. Just because running with a certain person looks good in the natural does not mean that it will actually benefit you or fulfill God's purposes in the spirit.

There is a great shift coming to the body of Christ. God is repositioning many, connecting different people with different ministries, realigning people and moving many people to different places. One person or one ministry cannot give you everything you need in order to continue to grow. When I was in school, from Kindergarten to when I graduated from college, I attended 7 different schools. It is the same way in the spirit. God will use many different avenues to continue our development.

Some of you have had the same mentor in your life for so long that you are no longer growing. Some of you have been planted in one ministry for so long that you need to glean from other teachings and anointings in order to move forward. This is why, in our personal ministry, my wife and I always encourage the people running with us to listen to other ministers' worship music, podcasts and teachings. We encourage those who run with us to read other ministers' books. Gleaning from many different trustworthy voices will help you to continue to grow and move forward.

You need intercessors. You need apostles and prophets around you. You need to get some people around you that will help you move forward. If you are going to move forward, you need to cut off your dead, broke friends and make them acquaintances. Pray for them and text them every now and then, to see how they are doing, but don't spend all your time with people who are not next level.

In 2 Kings 4, we find the story of the prophet Elisha and the Shunamite woman. This lady was a woman who took care of Elisha whenever he was in her town. After she had been taking care of him for a while, Elisha looked at her one day and said, "What can I do for you?" And she answered him and told him that she wanted a child. So Elisha prayed for her and prophesied over her that within a year, she would have a son. A year later, the woman gave birth to a son. My friends, Elisha was a next level friend to this woman because she had proven herself to be next level. You've got to get around some people who can open up dreams for you. You need next level friends who can open up dead wombs of your life and dreams.

Now when her son got older, he was out working in the field one day and something happened. He cried out and said, "My head, my head!" and then fell down dead. So the servant ran to the woman and told her that her son was dead and she looked at him like a mama does. She took her son, laid him up in his room, got on her donkey and started riding straight forward to find Elisha.

On her way several people tried to stop her, but she didn't slow her donkey down even a little bit. She just stuck her hand out, said, "It is well," and kept going straight forward to find the man of God. She didn't look to the right; she didn't look to the left. She just moved straight forward. If you want to do what you are called to do, you've got to be like this Shunamite woman and keep moving straight forward no matter what. You've got to get around next level people who won't try to stop you from moving forward.

Once she got close to where Elisha was, he saw her and sent Gehazi to go see what she wanted. But she didn't answer any of Gehazi's questions. She just said, "It is well." So they both went to Elisha. 2 Kings 4:27 says, "Now when she came to the man of God at the hill, she caught him by the feet, but Gehazi came near to push her away. But the man of God said, "Let her alone; for her soul is in deep distress, and the Lord has hidden it from me, and has not told me." So, Elisha told her, "Take my staff and lay my staff on the face of the child." But she replied, "I'm not leaving here until you leave with me."

This woman refused to leave without Elisha even though he had offered to send Gehazi and his staff with her. She knew that Elisha was the next level friend that had the power of God to bring forth her miracle. Some of you need to stop settling for good friends and look for your God-ordained friends. 2 Kings 4:31 says, "Now Gehazi went on ahead of them, and laid the staff on the face of the child; but there was neither voice nor hearing. Therefore, he went back to meet him, and told him, saying, "The child has not awakened." Imagine what would have happened if she had not insisted on the man of God coming himself!

Elisha went into the boy's room, stretched himself out over the boy and prayed. He did this two times and then called for the mother. Elisha called for Gehazi and said, "Call this Shunamite woman." So, he called her and when she came in to him, he said, "Pick up your son." So she went in, fell at his feet, and bowed to the ground; then she picked up her son and went out. The boy did not get up healed until Elisha went into the room. But the mom had her face set like flint because she knew who her next level friends were. Some of you are settling for good reports about your situations instead of God reports. Some of you need to stop settling and get away from those that do not have the power of God working in their lives. You need some next level friends!

Luke 6:12-13 says, "Now it came to pass in those days that Jesus went out to the mountain to pray, and continued all night in prayer to God. And when it was day, He called His disciples to Himself; and from them He chose twelve whom He also named apostles." Jesus stayed up all night in fasting and prayer to find out who He should be running with. Jesus prayed about who He was connected to.

When was the last time you connected with a new person and you fasted and prayed to see if you were supposed to be connected to that person? Whoever you run with can either pull you forward or pull you back. If we surround ourselves with people who are always moving forward, we will move forward. But if we surround ourselves with those who are not progressing, they will pull us back.

In Luke 6:13, Jesus called the 12 men He chose as His "disciples" but He recognized them as apostles. Apostles are builders. Apostles are people who naturally feel motivated to move forward. Jesus recognized the gifts in the 12 men He chose. He knew He needed to surround

Himself with those who were moving forward. In certain times of our lives, we will have to identify the gifts in those around us, to move them forward, and to move forward personally.

Steve Hill, the evangelist that helped lead the Brownsville Revival, taught many times about 3 different circles of people you have in your life. There is the outer circle of the multitude of people you come in contact with. The second circle which is slightly smaller is the circle of your acquaintances. And finally, there is a very small circle in the middle which is the inner circle. The people in your inner circle must be people you know you can trust.

We see Jesus practice this principle in His own relationships. Why did Jesus only pick 12 disciples? It was because He was very intentional about the men He surrounded Himself with. Then Jesus had His inner circle of the 3 disciples that were closest to Him, Peter, James and John. Jesus was even more selective with who He shared His most intimate plans and experiences with. This is why the Bible names John as "the beloved disciple."

Peter, James, and John were Jesus' next level friends. He entrusted revelation and experiences to these men that He entrusted to no one else. Matthew 17:1-2 says, "Now after six days, Jesus took Peter, James, and John his brother, led them up on a high mountain by themselves; and He was transfigured before them." Jesus had the 12 but only took 3 up the mountain with Him when He was going to be transfigured. Why did He only share this experience with those 3? He only took His inner circle with Him because they were probably the only ones who were ready for it. If you could be offended in Jesus' day, He would have offended you. He looked at the 3 and invited them to the mountain with Him and told the other 9 to stay behind. Jesus looked at the 9 and said, "You stay here. You're not next level right now. But you'll get there." And He only took the 3.

Once again, in Matthew 26, Jesus only took Peter, James and John with Him into the garden of Gethsemane. Jesus took his inner circle to the garden with Him knowing they would see a side of Him that no one else would get to see. When Jesus went into the garden of Gethsemane, the 3 in His inner circle saw Him in agony. Next level friends are the only ones you let into the most personal parts of your life. You must be able to discern who in your life is really for you. If you let people who are not next level friends into your toughest times, they will talk about you and use it against you, instead of being there for you. Next level friends are friends that will fast and pray for you, not talk about you.

You must run with people who have your best interest at heart. Amos 3:3 says, "Can two people walk together without agreeing on the direction?" Next level friends will help you move forward. If the jokers around you aren't going where you're going, get them out of your life. God will replace wrong relationships with next level relationships. Never try to force a relationship or alignment with someone, flesh driven alignments will never produce Godly oil or fruit. Allow God to bring the right people at the right time into your life and ministry. We must always keep God as our closest relationship. Who you run with can be a huge help or hindrance. Be careful who you run with!

Moving forward means moving to the next level. Your next level will require new Kingdom relationships and removal of those that may be holding you back. Those who were only acquaintances in past seasons may become some of the closest people to you as you move forward. However, as you go to the next level, those that were closest to you may become mere acquaintances. You may need to cut ties with some toxic people. You don't have time for doubters, manipulators or negative people. You need some next level friends. You must have a made-up mind to remove all toxic people from your life because you've got to move forward!

Many of you, the reason those doors of breakthrough and opportunity have not opened for you yet is because of the people standing next to you. Some of the people you are running with would drag you back if certain doors opened for you. There may be other types of people beside you that, if the door opened, going through it with you would destroy them. God loves everyone but He has something for you and something different for them. If you want those doors of opportunity and breakthrough to open, you must be running with the right people!

Builders and painters use scaffolding as temporary structures to get something specific accomplished. Scaffolding has a specific purpose but it is temporary. Some people in your life are like scaffolding. They're in your life for a reason and a season, just like scaffolding. That's why you must learn to discern what kind of relationship to have with people. Scaffolding friends will help move you forward in the right season. But once that season is over, they have to leave and you have to let them go in order to move forward.

Next level friends are not seasonal or temporary. These are what some people call "ride or die" friends. Next level friends will always help you move forward and will keep moving forward with you in every season.

In Acts 13, Paul and Barnabas were doing ministry. I love this story. It's an apostolic story. As they were out ministering, they were invited by the proconsul to come and minister to him. When Paul and Barnabas tried to come to minister to him, a sorcerer and false prophet, that the proconsul was friends with, kept them from doing so. Sometimes, the people closest to you will keep what God wants to do in your life from moving forward.

Acts 13:7-12 says, "The men opposed them, seeking to turn the proconsul away from the faith. But Paul, filled with the Holy Spirit, looked intently at him and said, "You son of the devil, you enemy of all righteousness, you are full of all deceit and you are a fraud. Stop making crooked the straight paths of the Lord? And now, the Lord is going to strike you with blindness." Next level people are people of power. Anyone can talk about Jesus all day, but the real question is, who can produce power? Ephesians 6:10 speaks of "the explosive power of God working in us and through us." When you pray you should expect and be ready for the power of God to be manifested.

Paul and Barnabas were operating in the power of God. They spoke to the sorcerer and he was struck with blindness. There was another man traveling with them named John Mark. Acts 13:13 says, "Now when Paul and his party set sail from there, John Mark, departing from them, returned to Jerusalem." John Mark stopped traveling with Paul and Barnabas after this demonstration of power. I don't know about you but if I see men of God walking in such great power, and I am remaining on the journey with them, I'm not leaving. I will finish the journey with them because I want to learn more about and personally experience what they are demonstrating. When the apostolic grace and power hit, John Mark got scared, turned around and left. John Mark was not next level.

Most people, when someone like John Mark tries to leave, they try to convince him not to. I've seen so many ministers quit moving forward trying to keep a few John Marks happy. When God is removing someone from your life, let them go. Just let them go! It's a hard thing to do but if you don't, you won't be able to move forward. You must learn how to discern who is next level and who isn't.

Who you run with in life makes all the difference. Running with people who are spiritually strong will keep you moving forward. Hebrews 6:12 says, "Imitate those who through faith and patience inherit what has been promised." Look around at the people you have in your life. Are these the type of people that when they encounter warfare or hard situations, push through? When people come against them or they are having a hard time financially, do they still keep moving forward? Or do they stop and quit? Next level friends are those who are spiritually strong. Run with people who have great faith and patience. Don't listen to people who try to hold you back with their negativity or "woe is me" mindset. You don't have time for them.

Next level friends are those that will say, "Come on! Get yourself up and push through." Surround yourself with people of faith. People of faith do not stop until they have laid hold of every promise and accomplished every assignment that God has for them. You need those kind of people in your life. Never settle for less than the fullness of what God has called you to. Never settle for people who are willing to settle for an average, comfortable existence either. You must refuse to be around anyone who is not a winner in life. You need to run with people who are next level. You need to run with people who are moving forward.

Next level friends are those that have been through hard times and keep moving forward with God. There are many people who go through something hard and want to just hangout on the sidelines of life. These sideline people will keep you from really living your life for God. Next level friends are people who are ready to run. This is why Proverbs 27:17 says, "As iron sharpens iron, so a man sharpens the countenance of his friend." It does not say, "One sharpens one and then he goes and does his own thing." This is not the way it is meant to be, my friends. Real friendships are ones where we sharpen each other.

The Lord told me this, "Grow close to people who have been through hard times and followed Me all the way through until they got their breakthrough. Align yourself with people who stay in the battle until they inherit the promises and the purposes that I have designed for them!" Who you run with in this season is very important. For many, this is the season you have been waiting for your entire life. Get around the right people and go after all that God has for you!

CHAPTER 7: RUNNING AFTER GOD

In ministry, I encounter people who have a word from God about their purpose, ministry, family, and business. They have prophetic words from God about so many things but they aren't doing anything with them. Many times, I will challenge people, especially people who want to run with me, by telling them, "I am going to do everything that God has called me to do in life. You are going to get to watch me run after God and fully do everything God has destined me to do. But, am I going to get to watch you do what God has called you to do? Or will I see you doing the exact same thing this time next year?"

Let me share a secret to success with you. Success never happens by accident. Imagine you are watching the Olympics and the world's greatest runners are lined up to compete in a race. In between two of these very skilled runners, there is an open lane. No one ever comes down from the stands and jumps into the open lane to start running in the race and win. That doesn't happen! Why? Because those runners are athletes who have spent years training and conditioning their bodies to run and their goal is to win that race. We will never win the race of life by accident. Like those high-level athletes, we must be focused, discipled and conditioned to be successful in whatever God has called us to. Success does not come by accident.

Psalm 31:2 says, "I run to you, God; I run for dear life!" When we are running this hard and fast after the things of God, we have to know how to sustain ourselves. The best long-distance runners do one vital thing that helps them run long distances: they pace themselves. Long-distance runners and sprinters run differently. Sprinters run hard and fast because speed is what is most important in that particular type of running. But long-distance runners are more concerned about making it to the finish line than how fast they get there.

Runners who run long distance pace themselves. If you want to run at a very fast pace, for a long period of time, you have to pace yourself. It's the same way in the spirit. If we truly want to accomplish great exploits for God, we have to be more focused on simply moving forward, not on how fast we're getting there. We don't want to just be people who run hard and fast after God for a season and then fizzle out. We're in this race until the end!

One way we can pace ourselves in the spirit is, most importantly, to keep our private time with God fresh every day. We have to have a daily time of reading the Word and a daily time of prayer and seeking the Lord's face. Hebrews 11:6 says, "God is a rewarder of those who diligently seek Him." There are times where I am constantly on the road traveling and preaching. But I also have times, where for several months, I don't travel very much. During those down times I am just cramming the Word in, studying, praying and just devouring the Word of God. I have to keep myself full of the Word of God, so that during those busy times, I'm sustained. When I don't have time to study for hours and hours, I can reach back into those times where I digested so much of the God's Word and draw from that.

You also have to have seasoned, experienced fathers and mothers in the spirit imparting into your life. You have to constantly have wise men and women of God speaking into your life. Also, attending conferences, reading books and listening to podcasts that have to do with the areas you desire to move forward in will help to sustain you as you run after God.

The religious culture has no idea what to do with people who don't fit their man-made mold. They usually tell people to sit down and be quiet, whereas apostles usually tell people to stand up and say what God has given them. Many people are looking for permission from a leader before they will move forward and go after their God-given dream. I love to tell people, "Go! Run after that dream that has been locked up inside of you for years."

Yes! You are free from religious bondage, if you choose to be. Galatians 5:1 says, "Let me be clear, the Anointed One has set us free—not partially, but completely and wonderfully free!" Yes, you are free to go live the life you know God has called you to live. Yes, you have permission to. Yes, God is telling you to run, and run fast, after everything He has called you to. Never let the religious system hold you back. Stop letting critical, dominating leaders push you around and hold you back.

My whole life I was told "No, no, no" by the religious culture. Now my apostle, Ken Malone, says, "Joe Joe, you and Autumn, go, go, go!" The freeing voice of a father gives us validation and permission to run hard after the Lord.

Understand this, while you are running after the things of God, you must maintain the structures and strategies that the Lord has given you. Being structured with what God calls you to, grows your capacity to receive more from the Lord. Once you have those God-given structures and strategies in place, whatever God has told you to do, run with it! Don't walk or stroll, you need to run! Whenever God says, "Go," you better get going!

As you run after God, the wind of the Spirit will get behind you and keep you going. When King David was anointed by Samuel in his father, Jesse's, house in 1 Samuel 16:13, it says that, "The Spirit of God entered David like a rush of wind vitally empowering him for the rest of his life." Whenever you step into something and God anoints you for it, the wind of God will empower you to keep running. You won't want to stop because you've got the wind and the power of God behind you, moving you forward.

Hebrews 12:1-2 says, "Therefore we also, since we are surrounded by so great a cloud of witnesses, let us lay aside every weight and the sin which so easily ensnares us, and let us run with endurance the race that is set before us." The Word of God is saying that God has a specific path that He has set before us. We each have a specific race that we must run, and if you are going to run, you might as well run fast! But, if you are carrying a bunch of weights, you can't run very fast.

As we run after God, endurance is so important. Endurance means to push through a difficult process without giving way. You're going to have to get a tenacity about you and make up your mind that you're not going to quit. You've got to decide to stay in the fight, no matter what the devil throws at you or how hard it gets.

2 Timothy 4:7 says, "I have fought the good fight, I have finished the race, I have kept the faith." If you are going to run and finish your race in life, you are going to have to fight the fight. When you're running after God and actually doing something impactful for the Kingdom of God, it is not going to be a leisurely stroll through the park, my friends. It's going to be the fight of your life. The devil is going to throw everything he's got at you. People may come against you, but you're going to have to fight the good fight of faith if you want to successfully finish the race. Anything worth having in life is worth fighting for! A glorious future and destiny in Christ is awaiting you, but you're going to have to fight for it!

Psalms 18:29 says, "For by You I can run against a troop, by my God I can leap over a wall." Another translation says, "By your help I have made a way through the walls of a structure that was shutting me in; by the help of my God I have gone over a wall." The roadblocks that have stopped you in the past are gone. You want to know the biggest roadblock you have? Your mind. You have to get your mind made up that you're going to move forward, no matter what! If you can get your mind made up and focused, there is no roadblock or wall that can stop you.

Breakthrough is your portion. I believe God is giving many people a powerful breakthrough anointing. So that wherever you go, and whatever you do, you will bring change. The anointing for breakthrough is coming and it will not just be one isolated breakthrough, it will be a sustained breakthrough. When you pray, Heaven and Earth shakes and moves because you are a child of God declaring the word of the Lord!

Forerunners are not called to go into a region and adapt to the climate. This is one of the real challenges that apostolic and prophetic forerunners often face. You may feel pressured to conform to the climate and to the culture, but you have to stay strong. Don't buckle under the pressure! You are called to challenge and radically transform the climate and culture, not conform to it. To bring a shift, you must pray radical prayers and stir yourself up in order to resist the pressure to conform to the status quo.

If you run after your God-given dreams, you will distance yourself from complacent people because they are the ones holding you back! Forerunners often outrun everyone in their community, city and region. This can sometimes be discouraging because you feel like you are running alone. But don't stop, forerunner! Forerunners must have a follow-through anointing. They must operate in a finishing anointing. You must be someone who starts and finishes seasons strong. I challenge you to dream big, run fast, and follow through! Everywhere you go, breakthrough will start to happen because through God you can break through the structures that have been shutting you in. Remember, breakthrough is your portion!

I want to share the story of where we get the term "marathon" with you. The name comes from the legend of Pheidippides, the Greek messenger. The legend goes that there was a group of outnumbered Greek soldiers who were fighting the Persian army. The Greeks somehow managed to drive back the Persians who had invaded the coastal plain of Marathon. An Athenian messenger, named Pheidippides, was dispatched from the battlefield to Athens to deliver the news of the Greek victory. After running about 25 miles to the Acropolis, he burst in and shouted to his fellow Greeks, "Nike! Nike! Nenikikamen!" which in Greek means, "Victory! Victory! Rejoice, we have conquered!" And, then, he fell over from exhaustion and died! Now, think about that.

2 Timothy 4:7 says, "I have fought the good fight, I have finished the race, I have kept the faith." If you are going to run and finish your race in life, you are going to have to fight the fight. When you're running after God and actually doing something for the Kingdom of God, it is not going to be a stroll through the daisies, my friends. It's going to be the fight of your life. The devil is going to throw everything he's got at you. People will come against you but you're going to have to fight the fight, if you want to finish the race. Anything worth having in life, you're going to have to fight for it.

What if that is what you were known for? What if for the next 25 years, you ran as hard and as fast as you could? What if at the end of your life, you could look back and know that you had successfully finished your course and that you gave your whole life to fully hitting your mark? I find that story so inspirational because Pheidippides, like the Apostle Paul, gave everything he had, never quitting or stopping, and fully hit his mark. He delivered the message that had been given to him, even though it cost him his life. You can do the same thing! Run after God and hit your mark. Run your race so you can look back upon your life with no regrets. You might just glance back at some point to find a remnant of passionate God-chasers running hard after Him with you!

About The Authors

Joe Joe and Autumn Dawson are the Founders and
Apostolic Oversight of ROAR Apostolic Network
and ROAR Church Texarkana. Their desire is to see
every believer fulfill their God-given destiny and live
life to the fullest in God. The Dawsons travel the
nation with a message of personal revival, freedom,
purpose and destiny. They reside in Texarkana,
Texas with their 3 children: Malachi, Judah & Ezra.

CHECK OUT THE OTHER BOOKS FROM JOE JOE DAWSON

40 P's Of The Apostolic
Kingdom Mindset
Destiny Dimensions: A 60 Day Devotional
Living Your God Sized Dream
Recipe For Revival

FOR MORE INFORMATION VISIT,
JOEJOEDAWSON.NET

CONNECT WITH US
SUBSCRIBE + FOLLOW

JOE JOE DAWSON
FACEBOOK

@JOE_JOE_DAWSONTXK
INSTAGRAM

@PASTORJOEDAWSON
TWITTER

JOE JOE DAWSON
YOUTUBE

@JOEJOEDAWSON
PERISCOPE

JOEJOEDAWSON.NET
WEBSITE

LIVING OUR *best* LIFE

MARRIAGE · FAMILY · LIFESTYLE

LIVINGOURBESTLIFE.NET

Roar Apostolic Network is a network of believers who are contending for revival and awakening. Our heart is to help train and equip every person and ministry that comes into alignment with us. We are called to walk in the fullness of God's authority and power while abiding in the Father's love. Our calling is to help others reach their God-given dreams and destiny. This network is built for a church, ministry, pastor, business person, intercessor, believer, etc. ROAR stands for Revival, Outpouring, Awakening, and Reformation.

For more information, visit roarapostolicnetwork.com

Roar Church is an Apostolic community of believers passionate about the Kingdom of God in Texarkana, Texas. It was founded in 2017 by Apostle Joe Joe & Autumn Dawson. Roar Church is a gathering of believers seeking the presence and power of God together. It is our desire for revival, outpouring, awakening and reformation to transform our region and see the Kingdom of God manifested in the earth.

For more information, visit roarchurchtexarkana.com

WEBSITES · BOOK DESIGN · GRAPHICS
MCFARLAND-CREATIVE.COM

All of the Dawson's books have been administrated by
McFarland Creative. McFarland Creative offers full book
facilitation that includes book editing, interior design,
formatting & cover design. We will take your vision for the
book inside of you and make it a reality. If you are
interested in sharing your words with the world,
email info@mcfarland-creative.com today!

CPSIA information can be obtained
at www.ICGtesting.com
Printed in the USA
BVHW041410270122
627358BV00010B/736